WINGS OVER
AFRICA

Susan Murray

WINGS OVER
AFRICA

*Wings Over Africa is a Biography of a very heroic man that flew his small plane (**The Auster**) from England to Southern Rhodesia, in Africa.*

During his Air Force training in Southern Rhodesia, he fell in love with this land of such great opportunities and decided even then he would one day return.

He returned to England after his training to do his peace for his country during the second world war.

Daniel Murray with his ex-war army buddy Fred Harris (who was no Air pilot) was to become his navigator during this exciting trip flying from England to Africa in his small aircraft he purchased after the second world war.

Just after the war things in England and Europe didn't look rosy enough for him to start civilian life with his wife and two small children and knowing what great opportunities there were in Africa convinced him to go ahead to make plans to return there with his family.

He met Fred when he was serving in the Army in his earlier years before he ended up as an Air force Pilot, they struck up a very good relationship as buddies over a mound of potatoes they were both assigned to peel.

All he had was a couple of maps, and compass, no radio or Dinghy's on board, Daniel's flying experiences and landings at some airstrips were quite "nerve wrecking".

This is a true story (in his very own words taken from his journals of ex Air force (Warrant Officer in Transport Command) Daniel Murray as he wrote about the sadness leaving his young wife and 2 young sons behind once more after the war as they bid their farewells at Barton Airfield in Manchester not knowing if they would ever be reunited again, and what they were to face ahead of them was both exciting and very tense.

Friendships along the way, excitement and fear they encountered including the threat with confiscation of his plane of which they made contingency plans for a quick getaway during the night to continue their very successful and exciting journey to Africa.

It never came to this in the end, however, as things turned out, but the plans were in place if they needed to use them!!

Their expedition took place in May 1947!!

(1)

As a boy I always remember having a passion in wanting to fly and become part of the Air Force in some way but it seemed it was not meant to be due to my height, as there were rules on height for flying and only being 5' 4" I didn't stand a chance at all, so reluctantly I recruited for the Army, which was the next choice, unfortunately not being happy with the Army, I persisted and persisted and after a long wait from the RAF making a decision, it came to light and I was sent off to Uxbridge, Middlesex for a pilot test and eventually I was to succeed.

My training period was either going to be Canada or Africa so, they decided on Africa where this whole story unfolds.

Whilst stationed in Southern Rhodesia I came to love this beautiful part of Africa with it's amazing beauty and perfect healthy climate for anyone to enjoy.

The white communities were mostly British ex colonials, so, the native people were taught the English-speaking language in the finest of ways which taught them very fluent English.

I noticed how the country was very relaxed hence the colonialist way of life, both immigrants and native people alike were always friendly, obliging, relaxed with no pressures, and always there to help.

I imagined life back in England where there was no hope for a good life just after the war, everywhere struggling to survive, no employment and all the rationing on foods.

Here in Africa, there was no sign of wars or aftermath of war, just tranquillity and a vast open area for opportunities.

I stayed with a beautiful family out there and met such wonderful people who eventually became very close friends to me.

After my training I was sent back to the United Kingdom to start my career and stint in the RAF.

I thoroughly enjoyed what I was assigned for and just loved to be flying it was like freedom to me just to be in the sky.

The Army was a boring job but also understanding that we all had a job to do but for me, I was unhappy in the army, although through this whole saddened war I was enjoying every minute of what I did.

I became a Chief Transport Commander and achieved much experience learning lots of new and interesting exercises throughout my time with the RAF.

My passion for the air and flying stayed with me forever!!!

Daniel Murray

Warrant Officer of Transport Command.

Royal Air Force

I still had Africa in my blood and could not shake this off so eventually after the war and a lot of planning which included purchasing an **"Auster Aircraft"** I decided to take my wife and family to Africa where I knew deep inside me was the best thing I could have done for us all to enjoy a happier life.

(2)

May the ninth 1947

At last the day had arrived, we had been awake half the previous night packing our bags with the most necessary of our requirements.

We could not carry a great deal for fear of overloading the little aircraft in which we were leaving the country that very morning in search of better opportunities further afield.

I had purchased an Auster a small aircraft for this venture and much red tape to go through before all was finalised.

After almost three months of preparation involving visits to scores of authorities, visits which entailed making long and tiresome journeys by road and rail to various parts of the country ,we finally had our Passports with the all-important visa's , the log books and the permits in our possession, all was ready for the "Off" so, with little fuss as possible we bid our families farewell.

We climbed into the aircraft, made a final taxing out to the downwind boundary of the airfield which was a sad business, and as we moved slowly across the field it was time to wonder if we would ever see those whom we had just left, those who are very dear to us and who would be waiting for news of us every day, and trusting in the plane as much as we were.

A few minutes later we were air borne and there was more for us to think about, details to attend to and the sadness of the previous few minutes was engulfed by a new beginning and fascinating interest, we were at long last en-route to Southern Rhodesia.

Dan Murray holding his propeller with Fred Harris. Ready for their expedition in 1947.

(3)

Spring was beginning to assert itself; the weather was ideal and after making a few circuits we headed for Derby.

We had a little business matter to clear up at Derby Airfield and had planned to land there but the heavy thaw after the snow had made several grass landing grounds unstable and we were uncertain of the actual state of the ground.

The short trip to Derby from Manchester was a mixture of all sorts of conditions and the first of these we experienced immediately after having passed over the centre of Manchester.

It wasn't really on track but we had flown around the town several minutes having a last look at the old firm where I was employed before resigning, then around the districts where friends resided and so, we were eventually a mile or two South East of the Town Centre when we noticed the "Smoke Haze" which had drifted from the old factories, the visibility was appalling and it was only with the greatest difficulty that we managed to keep a check on our position.

By the time we had reached Macclesfield the haze was behind us, then we had to climb over the snow-capped Derbyshire Hills, flooded areas were numerous and in many parts there was still more snow to thaw, we both remarked on the severity of the winter which was now waning and both agreed that it was the most bitter we had ever known, it wasn't just the snow falls, but also the icy winds and continuity of such conditions which had made the passing winter so unforgettable.

As much as the shortages of fats, bread and meat and above all the fuel crisis and the absolute despair of people without fires.

We and our families had been but a handful out of millions who had been without fires for days at a time.

Well, here we were leaving the winter and Manchester behind, and soon should land at our first call en-route, and within a short time we were cleaning up the last details with the people at Derby Airfield.

We were invited to a farewell lunch and could hardly refuse, but we didn't want to stay longer than necessary due to trying to make Limoges early in order to clear customs and carry on to Paris the same day.

(4)

We took off again within an hour of landing, not only had the wind changed direction since we left Barton, it had also strengthened considerably, and it was apparent that we could not hope to get to Paris until the following day.

Although the journey South was miserably slow, we had ample opportunity to see the English meadows and farms spreading out below us and a last glimpse of London as we passed just outside the 25-mile zone.

We crossed the Thames, saw departing ships and ships at anchor possibly arrived with valuable food stuffs, some in dock surrounded by busy nodding of cranes and in the distance another huge cloud of filth which had been belched from the town below.

We lingered along the South bank of this great river until we could almost see Limoges this was about 5.pm in the evening.

I made a special note of the time of crossing the coast in order to get an accurate ground speed check on reaching the other side.

There were only 21 nautical miles to go but it was our first hazard and the thought of choking an Auster was not very savoury, we had no means of survival should the engine fail us on this crossing.

The load on the aircraft was already high, and we just couldn't find any way of having a dinghy, so, it was only to be expected that whilst slowly passing over the water there was an uncomfortable silence.

Neither of us spoke for a while and then Fred trying hard to appear to be un concerned, confident and happy said *"The weather is good, that's one good thing"* it's as though all his thoughts immediately prior to speaking had been completely dismal until he suddenly agreed with himself, that at least there was one item which could be appreciated even if we were over the channel without a dinghy and then decided to say so.

Agreeing with a nod, I looked as far as I could both to the north and then to the south and it really was a most perfect day, the visibility was good, the sea was calm and sparsely dotted with small channel craft.

The white cliffs of Dover looked as if they had been newly whitewashed as they contrasted with the beautiful blue of the sea.

The French cliffs just south of Cap Gris Nez were still in the shade, the sun still being low in the East and looked dismal compared to the Dover Chalks but the beaches looked cool and inviting, they were all deserted in spite of their beauty, but it was still early in the year and the water no doubt would have been very cold indeed.

As soon as the French coast passed directly beneath us, we marked the exact spot on the map, noted the time, made a fair quick calculation and found the wind was from the Northeast at a speed of about 20 knots allowing for a drift to starboard of 2 or 3 degrees.

We altered course, this kept us very close to the coast, and we could fully appreciate the attraction which the French fishing villages have for the English tourists.

The little coves and creeks with the numerous rowing boats lifted high and dry.

One could easily imagine how easy it must have been in the old days to load up with the odd dozen kegs of wine or rum to get across to England for big profit.

The very appearance of the places seemed to suggest romance, smuggling, adventure and something different from most coastal resorts.

We had not spoken for a while but we each turned to say something and the shouting into each other's nearest ear began.

Fred broke the silence of it and could be termed as such *"smashing isn't it"* I replied with an *"eh"* he again repeated *"smashing isn't it"* I said *"yeah I think so too"* Fred answered with a *"what"* I just simply said *"yeah"* Fred replied with an *"oh"*. After that point we decided to let the engine have its own way and make all the noise.

The scenery again was the main attraction of the moment with an occasional glance at the map, then at the compass, oil pressure gauge etc, most of my attention was given to admiring the French countryside.

The coast had gradually passed from view and within a short time we should be seeing the notorious "River Seine"

Visibility was slightly deteriorating, and some 10 miles ahead looked to be rather dull, but we had only a few miles to go and I thought we might not encounter any rain.

As we neared Paris weather conditions became still more dull and we realised that the storm which by now was quite apparent, was centred just South of the capitol.

The Eiffel Tower came into view, and we circled it whilst Fred took a couple of snaps, but the light was very poor, and the effort achieved little success.

Owing to the storm we had little time to afford and there for missed the opportunity of seeing the straight tree lined boulevards of beautiful Paris as we would have liked and without wasting any further time, went in to land...

This was our first foreign port and our first experiences of the difficulties we were likely to have at all places where the English language was not predominant.

(5)

By the time we had submitted names and papers to the customs the rain had started and was beating down in torrents, everybody had sheltered indoors leaving the landing field a deserted soaking wilderness, even a young Frenchman who had been in a light little Kite, showing off to a bunch of French beauties had beat a hasty retreat from his cockpit, probably earning his luck at having his success interrupted so rudely by the sudden change in the weather and all his bevies of feminine's deserting him so abruptly leaving him to descend from his throne without having a single admirer.

The storm cleared within the hour, and we were soon heading South but it was difficult map reading because of the very hilly country and the low altitude of which we were forced to fly owing to low cloud.

We had to keep below the cloud in order to keep a check on position and in fact the cloud became so low that we had to resort to flying the last 30 or 40 miles along valleys.

The low clouds and strong air currents caused many uncomfortable bumps but at least it was interesting, and we put down at Limoges in the late afternoon.

Again, the snag of only having a very limited knowledge of French was making it rather awkward for us until an ex-paratrooper who had been stationed in England during a period of the war years came to our rescue.

We became very friendly in quite a short time and after attending all the necessary arrangements, he invited us to tea.

Within 15 minutes of entering his car we were entering his beautiful home situated on high land overlooking Limoges and surrounded by beautiful vineyards, groves, and orchards in blossom and a tumbling brook making its way to lower levels.

We happened to be their first guests since our friend, and his wife first occupied the house only a few weeks previously and with a pre-war out of tradition we made a toast to the young and happy couple.

The visit was originally tea only but after chatting about the parts of England familiar to our host, we accepted his invitation to have dinner and spend the night at his beautiful home.

His wife was Estonian and most charming, but she could only understand the odd word or two of English, and this rather complicated matters since it became the duty of Mr Solomon (our host) to translate from Estonian to English and although he had a fairly good knowledge of both these languages, being a Frenchman his own language was naturally French.

It was here at this delightful place that we had our first sample of high class French dinner and before half the courses had been served, I felt as though, if I ate one little bit more I would die, it was most embarrassing to have to refuse about the last 3 courses, but for the life of me, I just couldn't keep pace.

Fred fared much better than myself and coped a little bit longer than I, and he also managed to drink more, but before 9pm in the evening when we retired to our room, he was very near to being sozzled on the rich red wine and slept like a drugged grizzly bear, sawing the beams up wholesale.

The next morning was very fresh with a slight breeze, rustling the leaves outside the open window, but when I looked out the sky was so grey that I had my doubts about being able to leave Limoges that day, but we preferred not to impose on the hospitality that had been shown to us and so, went down to the airfield to ascertain whether take-off was advisable or not.

By the time we arrived the cloud had disbursed considerably and after our awkward struggle with words Mr Solomon humbly requested the possibilities of giving him a short flip in the aircraft, the very least I could do to show our appreciation for all he had done was to grant him his wish, and with no further ado he was sitting in the cockpit waiting for the "off" despite of all his encouragements he just couldn't persuade his wife to accompany him, and, perhaps it was for the best because from the moment we left the ground we were pitched about much more than I expected.

Although we had been up for only a few minutes, he was pleased to be getting down again but he thoroughly enjoyed seeing his home from the air and, I was glad to be able to please him.

The re-fuelling had been done the previous evening

so, there was only the flight plan to submit and the signatures to be added to the logbook etc and soon bidding Limoges and our wonderful hosts goodbye!!!

(6)

That day, the third day of our trip we hoped to get to Perpignan a few miles north of the Eastern extremity of the great Pyrenees, 50 miles South of Limoges, but the weather became much worse quite contrary to the forecast obtained through Limoges from Toulouse and by the time we reached Toulouse we had had enough, the visibility and low heavy clouds made it very unwise to continue, and the rain was beating down as we went into Toulouse for shelter from the very unstable elements.

As we put the aircraft into the hanger, the storm broke and sheets of rain driven by a 45 mph wind drenched everything before it, so, the prospects of leaving that day were out of the question so, we very reluctantly paid our fees and asked for a taxi.

Again an English speaking French gentleman came to our assistance and phoned to a taxi company for conveyance to town, this came at last driven by an old man with a typical "Old Bill" moustache but in spite of his comically and unkempt appearance, he was only perhaps in his late thirties and was accompanied by a "Post Card" type French woman who was evidently much younger than he and who appeared to be proving to us that her presence was merely for the purpose of showing his fairs of which the French girls still had plenty of "Oomph".

Obviously he was under the impression we were either wealthy tourists or mugs, and having been asked to take us somewhere for accommodation, he took us to the best Hotel in the town "The Grand", this was most luxuriously bedecked with divans and chairs and the fittings were of the very best, so, we naturally fought shy as we expected heavy expenses, we enquired at the desk the cost of a room for two and surprisingly was amazingly low, so, after consulting an attendant who spoke English perfectly but with an American accent only to discover he was actually a French Canadian.

We concluded that the best and economical thing for us to do was to sleep at the Grand but dine at a restaurant recommended by our new acquaintance, situated conveniently within ten minutes' walk from the hotel.

We only took a few minutes to wash and change and made for the restaurant, mentioning the name of our friend the attendant as per his advice, we were soon confronted by a menu which was most confusing, so, we made it quite clear that all we wanted was a substantial meal, within minutes we were served with hors d'oeuvres , the courses which followed were numerous and typically French but before half way through the meal our appetites were appraised so, when the cherries were brought to the table it was more than either of us could face, so, we just sat and talked and criticized the patrons who seemed to be able to eat indefinitely, oblivious of the amounts they were consuming.

Feeling quite full and contented we tried to estimate

the cost of our meal but when we had the cheque handed to us, we were both well below the figure, food was a reasonable price and would evidently be the most in-expensive item during our journey through France.

The weather was still very un-settled and for three days we had to stay put and only ventured away from the hotel as far as the restaurant. and several times we were caught in showers, but it was the very high winds and very low cloud that concerned me the most.

On the third day we encountered difficulty when trying to change travellers cheques and without the aid of the British Consulate we might have to stay until we had arranged to have money sent out from England, but he nobly came to our rescue in a very unique way and made it possible for us to pay our hotel bill and proceed by taxi to the airfield.

Strangely enough it was the same taxi driver, but his female companion of our previous trip was conspicuously absent, at least she had provided us with a subject of discussion, although many times the same subject unaccountably became the current type of conversation.

Conversation of great interest was very limited due to the type of trip we were doing with only 2 people , not knowing very much about each country and ignorant of their people and cultures and due to very little time we had in each place was disappointing to us but one day we may return as proper tourists wanting to learn more.

As we reached the airfield the weather gave a drastic change for the worse so, once more we were back in the taxi returning to where we left from, we had checked out of the last hotel so, we were forced to look for another, with good recommendations from the taxi driver we booked into another hotel not too far from the last one for another night and luckily this particular one was very reasonable and quite smartly furnished, we were by this stage getting accustomed to hotel living and it was only a matter of minutes before we felt perfectly at home.

After dinner we had coffee in the lounge at the invitation of a young couple who had overheard our English and knowing a little themselves were anxious to talk.

They were very helpful and certainly very friendly, so, before the evening was over, we had all become really chummy, and the following evening we accepted an invitation to accompany them to a smart cafe below which a cabaret' and dance was in progress.

We went downstairs and stayed for half an hour or so, wine, champagne, vermouth, gin and every mentionable drink was obtainable there, but we drank very little and were quite content to merely watch and listen.

Music was of the Lullaby class, sentimental and soft and the atmosphere of the room blended with the dim lighting, quiet shuffling, whispers and faint sounds of laughter.

In a shadowy corner were a very much "in love" couple.

Opposite to them were a gang of slicks drinking champagne like water as though they had money to burn, every female who entered caused all their eyes to be turned towards the stairs leading down to the den as it was called and all their heads were put together to whisper approval or disapproval, their drowsy eyes signified that they were in no condition to disapprove of anyone wearing feminine attire.

We didn't stay very long so, made for the hotel with the object of having sufficient to be feeling fit for early departure but

It didn't quite work out like that, we had to spend the following day loafing about locally, watching the wretched clouds roll by, and avoiding the leaves and dust as it swirled down the streets which was lashed about by the gusts.

We were miserable that day, 6 days had been lost out of the eight days we had been away from home, so, in desperation to avoid melodrama we voted on seeing a film show that evening, whether it was in French or not, at least we might see an English news reel we thought, so, we strolled along the local picture house to make a few enquiries, the film was definitely French , but there was a news-reel , the show started, we thought he said at 7.30 pm.

Dinner was at 7.00pm so we just had nice time to eat then, at 7.30pm we were there at the pay-box with not a soul insight apart from a fireman with an axe in his belt plus a brass helmet which was very much too big for him of which he preferred to twiddle rather than wear.

I think he knew he looked a fool, we probably also looked foolish to him for we were uncertain what to do, he approached us in a officious manner as though he knew that we were at a complete loss so, with an attempt to disown him of his spontaneously achieved over confidence, we walked past him as though he didn't exist , entered a swing door through which a young woman had just passed, there wasn't any sign on the door, otherwise we would have been dubious and kept away from it, but through the doorway we went and found ourselves in a huge room resembling a barrack room rather than a cinema yet the screen at one end was proof without a doubt.

There was no covering on the floorboards only wooden forms like those seen in a suburban park were set in rows so close together that the smallest of person's wouldn't be able to move a leg once seated.

A balcony of sorts seemed to have the most expensive of seating, so, we bobbed out again and by this time the ticket clerk was on duty in her little box, the dearest seats were 10 francs each so we got 2 of these and went upstairs, all was plain wood and not the least bit comfortable, at least being the first in we had a choice of seats.

The lighting was poor as small gas jets were burning at intervals along the wall and immediately above the flickering flames were huge dirty patches surrounded by deposits of soot which looked like it formed over a long period of time.

I was watching a couple enter from down below and thought I saw a movement down on the small stage at the back of which the screen was mounted.

Looking about me, I again thought I saw some movement down at one corner of the stage, I looked carefully " see that Fred"? I said, giving him a quick nudge. "What, where?" he asked looking down to where I was now pointing, just then a youngster entered the door nearest the corner of the stage and quite plainly we could see a rat scamper hurriedly across the whole length of the stage and disappear through a gap between the curtain and wall.

We both started laughing because it really was an amusingly pokey little place, but the couple seated directly below us did not know why we were laughing and stared strangely up at us probably thinking that we were laughing at their expense, it so happened that the fireman had also entered and was giving us the once over, when I looked again he was still watching us perhaps because there were no others to watch.

When I was leaning over to one side fumbling in a pocket for matches, I had already got a cig between my fingers as I came across the match box, I placed the cig to my mouth looking at him as I did so.

Up the stairs he bounded towards me and as he started his blathering, I realised something was forbidden, so, I gave him as friendly a smile as I could muster under the circumstances, collected the cig which I had offered to Fred and replaced them in the box. I was thankful that it happened early before the place became packed.

We had been waiting 25 minutes when the show started with a French travel film, it was boring whilst it lasted, but it was only short followed immediately by a Walt Disney cartoon, everybody roared with approval with the familiar introduction so we were delighted too, but soon I realised that I had recently seen that particular film, I enjoyed it, however but I was wondering what was going to be next when another cartoon immediately followed the first and "whoops" of laughter and hand cheering emphasized the popularity of these cartoons.

We were at an advantage up to now because of the English dialogue, I was feeling as pleased as punch, but when the third one followed, we were both shrieking with laughter as though we had backed a winner. This sort of thing repeated itself 8 times in all then during the ninth Disney Film I was as happy as a proverbial pig.

We agreed we had had a good shillings worth of entertainment and didn't give two hoots what the remaining film was, it's a good job we didn't because it was so dull, the newsreel which we were assured was to be included in the show never appeared, in fact none of the information we had received ,proved to be correct.

At the end of the show it seemed judging by the number of children accompanied by adults that it was a special evening when the children of the community were catered for, I enjoyed that evening and so did Fred, the very moment we stepped outside we lit cigs, it was a great relief after sitting through the last film without being able to smoke.

During the short walk home, during supper and right until we retired that night we were talking and laughing about the way things turned out at the cinema and from then on circumstances seemed to improve for us.

(7)

We didn't bother about getting out of bed early the next morning, partly because we had been disappointed by the weather so many times now that we were getting fed up by the idea, but mostly because we didn't waken until about 8am and hadn't arranged to have an early call.

The wind was still strong but was in the right direction for us, we settled the account after breakfast, went and packed our bags and bundled off to the airport hoping we would be able to take off, straight to the met office we went and one look at the chart was sufficient.

The wind was coming from the North and would be on our tail, but it blew along the Pyrenees and out to sea at a velocity of 60-80 mph, this was too much for us and there was no alternative but to wait until the wind dropped, we couldn't cross the Pyrenees for they were too high for us although it wasn't far round, yet it was because the wind also went round that the wind speeds were high.

There was nothing else for it but to be patient, we sat down and had a drink in the buffet, we looked at the map as we had done many times.

Through the window we could see the snow caps of

the high range, which was causing us so much delay, so, looking down at the map again we decided not to return to Perpignan for rooms

but to go in the opposite direction along the main road to a small place called River slate's' it would possibly be a quaint place with lots of interesting features, so, we set off walking the 3 miles with only the bare necessities with a one night's stay in a bag, the rest of our baggage we left at the airport under lock and key.

The general direction of the place was to the north; the strength of the wind was even then increasing rapidly.

We approached a signpost which said that River Slate's' was 1 mile distant but leaning and pushing against a 50 mile per hour wind was no easy matter, but anyway we had plenty of time.

We sat down for half an hour smoking and nattering and chewing grass and cursing the mountain range which we could see distantly a few miles to the south of which was the cause of our delay ,we were feeling more than a little weary but we knew that the sooner we get to the village the sooner we would be able to rest in comfort, have food and enjoy the first sip from a glass of cool drink and I always think that the very first sip is always better than the rest.

Half-heartedly we got on the move again, plodding on as though we didn't care whether we got there or not.

There was nothing of interest along the way, the lonely road was very similar in appearance to the average English country lane, but it was very noticeable that the hedgerows were much more advanced in growth than those we had seen in England only a few days before.

It must have taken us over half an hour to walk the last mile, but it might have been the sign post that fooled us like they sometimes do, but it was probably the way we dawdled along, kicking stones, throwing at posts and acting more like tired kids returning from an all-day "birds nesting" expedition.

As we strolled into the village square, I felt that I had been walking for several days, all I wanted was a good cool drink, dinner and sleep.

We found a place but not without a little difficulty making the local folk understand what it was we were wanting as it appeared that visitors were rarely seen there so, therefore no attempt was made to cater for such.

Following directions of an old man we saw loitering around the corner of a building, we came across a somewhat dilapidated Cafe come Hotel in the making which was really an old house still undergoing alterations from the aftermath of the war, so, we were shown to a double room overlooking a row of backyards containing small gardens, hen pens, clothes lines, wash tubs, heaps of rubbish, piles of firewood and almost every conceivable form of junk, it was hardly a picturesque view, but to see everything that could be seen from the little window was almost an education in itself.

Food was ordered immediately and a quick wash was sufficient preparation and soon we were shown to the time of profound apologies to a dowdy, musty smelling room and asked to make ourselves comfortable on a battered old couch littered with torn newspapers, kids comic papers, crumbs, pieces of old clothing rammed into one end and, which was already occupied by an underfed scraggy looking cat.

Assuring a nonchalant air of "Oh, that's alright, anything will suit us" we seated ourselves on it and with a knowing glance at each other, tried to convey the impression that we were well satisfied and hadn't even noticed the filth which surrounded us.

Three children, a dog, two cats and we were left in the same room when the woman of the establishment departed to prepare a meal.

The dog was sniffing in a very unfriendly manner first at my legs and then at Fred's, then the cat after being removed from the couch was doing its utmost to return to the same warm spot from which it had been ejected, the kids were quietly giggling and whispering between themselves, we just sat and looked about and every glance at the kids who were constantly scrutinising us brought forth a new outburst of the aggravating tittering.

When the plates of food were placed on the table that had been drawn up before us, it was a great relief in more ways than one.

Had the kids been English we could have passed some appropriate remark but, under the circumstances there was nothing we could say in the way of friendly conversation.

The woman must have sensed the discomfort we were suffering and instantly began bundling the kids out with her as she returned to the kitchen and, we were left alone but for the two cats which had started to me-ow and were clawing up at the couch and the legs of the huge table for the want of something to eat, the dog had followed the kids.

The meal consisted of fried eggs and a few slices of cold salt meat, there were a couple of slices of very dark bread each and a jar of jam was on the table, coffee followed which tasted like burnt wood so, we were not too happy, then we stepped outside into the fresh air.

(8)

On our way into the square we had noticed a small beer house at the corner of a narrow street, so, we made for this place since it was the only one we had seen, the room we entered was small but cosy looking with a few small tables each surrounded by three or four comfortably shaped chairs, a table quite close to the door was occupied by about half a dozen people plus extra chairs having been drawn up and they were chatting in an easy manner as though they had all been meeting there every day for years, an assortment of wine bottles, fruit drinks etc were in the centre of the table and there was quite an assortment of glasses surrounding the bottles, the most popular of the drinks was wine, but we had tried the popular French wines in other places and were not impressed.

We seated ourselves comfortably and did what we could to try to make the man who stood slightly leaning over the table in askance that we would appreciate two cool fruit drinks or mineral waters, as usual we failed to be sufficiently explicit and two bottles of which the crown tops had been removed were placed before us, the contents looked gassy and looked invitingly refreshing but we soon discovered that it was ordinary tasteless soda water, he saw our disappointment and no doubt expected it, he came forward quickly and raising his eyebrows as a sign of request said *"Beer"? "Please"* was our brief answer, where upon he smartly collected our unemptied bottles, hurried to the counter and brought forth two ice cool half pints of ale, I still would have preferred something sweeter, but it was good and satisfying, we were enjoying it which pleased him.

He was watching us intently and was apparently self-debating on the advisability of sitting at our table and making an attempt at chatting to us, for suddenly he came over, turned a chair round with its back to the table and sat down casually with his arms folded on the chair back. *"Where in England where you come?"* he asked, pleasantly smiling across at us. *"Manchester"* I said, *"Do you know Manchester"?* Fred asked, almost at the same time on hearing this his eyes lit up, the smile broadened, his expression inferred that he had found a clue for which he had been searching all his life.

Snapping his finger and thumb together he jumped up from his chair, hurried behind the counter, we watched him as he stood on a box or something and unhooked from the wall a framed photograph which was hanging above a display cabinet. Still wearing his happy smile, he brought this over to us.

He went on to say, *"Here I was born in Salford which was once a borough of Manchester and I lived there for 25 years during my schoolboy days until I went to live elsewhere, I was a keen supporter of Salford Rugby League team."* The photograph was of the Salford Rugby Team which made a tour of France in 1936 and beat

Perpignan 52 points to nil, autographs of players

were on the back of the photo and of the team manager at the time, Lance Todd.

This was very interesting indeed, here we had travelled to a remote corner of France and found direct connection with the town of my bachelor days when the main topic in Salford was always the progress of the lads of the local rugby team.

Manchester have never had a rugby league team and, Salford which was once a borough of Manchester had the best team in the league.

All the players in the picture were familiar to us, as this fast became apparent to the others in the inn, we became quite the centre of attraction, some of the players who opposed the Salford team were sent for and soon we were shaking hands with them too.

Some of them who had recently joined the company were able to understand us, and so conversation was made much easier as a result.

One member of the Inn keeper's family brought a neat scroll and some medals and placed them carefully on the table. I opened the scroll, it was from General Eisenhower to the Inn keeper and was a message of thanks for the valuable assistance rendered during the war, in that he successfully concealed and then guided over the Pyrenees across the Spanish border at tremendous risk to himself and his family no fewer than 54 civilians who were being hunted by the Germans.

This was a wonderful thing, and he was a very proud man. We each shook his hand warmly if only to show our own appreciation of his courage.

The evening was short, and out in the street again

the air had become noticeably chilly, the gale had dropped but sudden gusts continued to whip up the dust.

The place became desolate with the approach of darkness, there was no reason for us to stay outdoors, no scenery to admire and in fact no interesting feature at all, so we turned in happy that there were prospects of departure.

(9)

The morning was bright; we were in good spirits again as we started off to walk back to the airfield.

There was a heavy due on the hedgerows, the grass sparkled as the sun rays reflected from the tiny drops of water adhering to the blades, ornamented by silken cobwebs covered with glittering sequins.

The birds seemed happy, spring was certainly in the air, and the walk back seemed not the slightest trouble.

There wasn't a breath of air, and everything looked peaceful and quiet, only the "tromp, tromp" of our feet and the twittering of the birds broke the stillness of the morning.

Neither of us spoke until we got nearer to the drome and then the atmosphere changed as we began to discuss the future departure.

As we walked through the gate, we could clearly see that the aircraft had been moved out of the hanger in anticipation of our take- off and a brief visit to the met room put us in still higher spirits.

We learnt that a wind would be right on our tail as soon as we got over the sea and that it was expected to increase in strength up to about 40 mph these conditions were similar right down the coast of Spain, so we expected to make very considerable progress during the next ten hours which, in fact we did.

At first, we were bumped about quite a lot, but the air gradually became more settled as we left the Pyrenees behind and, it was an enjoyable trip the whole way down to Barcelona, the picturesque coast being in view continuously.

We stayed in Barcelona but a very short time as we had difficulty in persuading the officials to allow us to continue through Spain, it appeared that strictly speaking we were officially only allowed to enter Spain on the condition that we left the same day.

We had planned to call at Valencia and Grenada and then on to Gibraltar to be able to get there that same day and the only other alternative was for us to return to France, we just couldn't turn back like that, so, we did our utmost to convince those concerned that we would be able to clear Spain that evening quite easily, although we were informed that in the event of us "not clearing" we were likely to have our aircraft impounded.

We decided getting on route again as quickly as possible and seeing if we could discover a "loophole" by which we could bluff our way through, we did.

Soon we reached Valencia and although the airfield at Barcelona was smart looking and well organised - especially in the restaurant where food, fruit and drinks of every kind were most plentiful-Valencia was equally as pleasant to visit.

We had no trouble here at all and no awkward

questions were asked at the Met office.

We learned that the wind had not altered much, and what was very interesting was the fact that the wind had backed slightly and was even more favourable than before for crossing the Med to Algiers.

If we took this way out we would avoid infringing any laws, the distance wasn't too much but, we had no earthly chance if the engine failed or if we even drifted very much to part of our desired track, there was every chance of missing the headland and continuing far out to sea where we would most certainly be doomed !!

We considered these points carefully, but the wind seemed to be just right, and there didn't appear to be any reason why it should alter in either direction or strength and since no drift would be expected, it looked as though it was much more advisable to head for Algiers than to go to Grenada where we would possibly meet with trouble from the authorities.

The only other snag with taking the Algiers route was the time factor and, if the wind strength did decrease appreciably, we would be approaching Maison Blanche, the Algiers airport during darkness, and I know the place to be adjacent to some high ranges of hills.

Negotiating these without blind flying instruments wouldn't be very pleasant, but as I said before, the wind wasn't likely to change at all, and if taking off at the time intended, we should make the North African Coast just before dusk.

The following day was Sunday the day of "Bull Fights" in Spain and we had hoped for an opportunity to see one of these as well as a chance to see some of the beauty of Spain but it wasn't to be as due to the circumstances and with no time to spare we hurriedly left Spain but not without first calculating carefully and accurately the course to steer.

(10)

This crossing of the Med was the biggest gamble we had yet taken, because we were not in any way equipped for such a trip but we had every confidence of the air worthiness and reliability of the aircraft and as we could see it, nothing but sheer bad luck could prevent us from reaching Algiers safely.

I remember some of my thoughts as we headed out over the water, not only were we taking a chance on our own lives, but the possible future of our dependants was also in the balance.

We began to talk lightly of possibilities which could spell doom to us , but we occasionally spoke seriously and kept a very close look out for any ships towards which we may be able to glide should any aircraft failure arise, ships were very few indeed and far between but when one did appear it gave a sort of relief as though it wouldn't matter very much if the worst did come to the worst.

Whilst a ship was insight there was always that possibility of being pushed up and whilst none could be seen it was a matter of watching the instruments, listening to the engine for any unusual sounds, passing some humorous remarks or other, scanning the wide expanse of water , and looking around the blue sky for other aircraft, for even the sight of another plane would have been a potential straw, and so the time passed and all was going well.

According to the map we would be seeing a couple of islands, possibly some thirty or so miles to port, and since the afternoon sun was on our southbound side and visibility was not quite 25' miles, at least there was every chance that we would see them.

We did see them eventually and we were much closer to them than we should have been, this meant that the wind had backed to blow from the southbound side, and I had to calculate a new course.

It appeared to be necessary to make an alteration to southbound of 8 degrees, and although it seemed to be rather a lot, I have long since learned that calculation is much more reliable than mere judgement or fancy, so we made the alteration and headed slightly west of the first course.

We were getting accustomed to this over water flying, the engine sounded perfect, weather was excellent and there wasn't a ripple in the air, and it was easy to steer accurately, and we had every confidence seeing Algiers on time.

I was slightly dubious about the wind and made frequent checks on the wind lanes showing on the sea, but the drift we had, seemed to be very consistently to port, and only slight too, and there was every reason to believe that a further alteration of course would be un-necessary.

As time went on, we marked on the map our

approximate position over the water, and according to our airspeed we just about covered half the distance when we noticed a faint suggestion of smoke directly ahead of us.

Visibility was so beautifully clear that the slightest blemish on the blue expanses of sea and sky could be picked up quite easily.

The wind proved to be at least 50 miles per hour, for it took us every minute of half an hour to reach the cause of the smoke.

It was a smallish craft of some ten thousand tons or so, painted white, all above the Plimsoll appeared to be a passenger carrying ship although there were also indications of freight carrying judging by the general appearance of the fourth deck.

She was flying a French flag and was heading South/Southeast almost the very same course as us.

We noticed that the smoke from the funnel was showing a slight drift to port, and the wash of the water also indicated that the wind was slightly from the Southbound side, which verified the need for heading a little to Southbound but the drift didn't seem much so, we again altered course, this time by 4 degrees to port having us with an allowance of 4 degrees of port drift.

We often looked back to see the ship for a last time, and we were hoping to see another before it disappeared below the horizon, but the remaining wisps of smoke had eventually vanished from view, again the limitless blue of water and sky were all that could be seen outside the aircraft.

We felt more and more confident as time went on

and we even tried a little sing song, but with the noise of the engine and the rushing of air past the open windows it was more like two solo's than a duet, since each of us could not hear the voice of the other.

Everything was going smoothly and we felt as though we had no worries in the world, and Fred decided to write a letter home thinking it would be rather unique to write whilst over the med and anyway it was , considering that before setting out from home he had never been in the air except for a couple of trial flips lasting no more than a few minutes.

I was content to watch for the coast appearing and according to my calculations it should be coming up soon.

Perhaps we were too far to port and were heading out to sea again having possibly misjudged the headlands, this was 300 miles from Valencia, I decided that we were not travelling fast enough to be more than 300 miles from Valencia and that patience was all that was required.

It was now getting a bit late though and we did want to get there before sunset, nothing in view ahead but as I looked out towards the sun I could see the high hills of the North African coast, but I couldn't yet see as I announced this fact.

Fred put his writing material away as though there wasn't a minute to spare, although we were still too far away to be able to ascertain exactly what part of the coast we could see, but anyway, land was in sight and that was something.

The sun was quite low by now and we could see the

red lights of the Maison Blanche - the airfield at Algiers - flashing out the letters of identification, and we were no more than 5 miles to Southbound of our intended track.

We were pleased as punch to have successfully achieved the long trip round Gibraltar for we had saved at least 3 days and made a very appreciable saving in fuel and expenses too.

It took us just 3 hours from the time of take off until the actual landing at Algiers, an average speed of 94 mph, we felt very satisfied.

It was getting quite dark as we taxied in, and we had to use navigation lights for the first time!!

We had a meal in the airfield buffet but then we discovered that although Algeria is a French territory, the French Franc was not the currency there.

We had plenty of French francs which we had purposely acquired for use in Algiers, but we had no Algerian currency.

We explained the position having had our notes refused, and a sympathetic attendant behind the counter offered to lend us some Algerian money until we changed some of ours.

There was no accommodation at the airfield, so we went into town, 15 miles on a bus belonging to Air France civil airline service and were shown to a hotel by a member of the staff of Air France.

At the hotel we had to offer French francs and at first were refused, but we had no other currency and finally the francs were accepted.

I was carrying a huge suitcase, a large service type pack and a brief case and the perspiration simply poured out of me.

Our guide gave us to understand that we only had to walk a short distance from the bus to the hotel, but it was over a mile, and I was just about "all in" by the time I dropped the kit on the floor near the reception desk.

There wasn't a breath of wind now, and the heat was oppressive, my hands were clammy I was aching all over, hot and sticky round the neck and I could feel my vest clinging to my back, the sweat even in my shoes, this was a devil of a change from a week ago when the air in England was crisp and dry and, part of the airfield at Derby was unserviceable because of the drifts of snow and the bogs caused by the thaw.

Once inside the hotel room around 8 floors up, we relaxed and ordered something to drink, and, spent the evening idly chatting after having bathed and refreshed ourselves.

No matter how tired we felt we were wanting to chat and chat.

The packing and unpacking of the bags were becoming monotonous yet we would have to do it many times before reaching Southern Rhodesia.

The choice of beds was a subconscious affair of just dumping the bags near a bed which made the decision, I sprawled full length on one of the beds and was content to wait for the bathroom.

Gazing up at the intricate design on the ceiling, my thoughts hazily drifted back to happy days gone by, thoughts of my wife and the first year of married life, the first holiday we spent together touring Cornwall and Devon, with our next-door neighbours, it was a delightful vacation.

I began to think of the earliest train of events since the outbreak of the war and how step by step I came to be in a position to travel out by air.

First the army life of a recruit when life away from home was unbearable and, the many times I had managed to slip off after duty to hitch hike back to a couple of hours of "the life of a civilian".

The transfer from Army to RAF and all the binding and red tape it involved; the final acceptance as a pupil pilot and then an entirely new, interesting and fascinating phase of my life began.

It was during the first stage of my army training that I first became acquainted with Fred.

We were very raw, we were amongst a batch of others detailed to peel potatoes, we struck up a friendship which went on to outlast the war, although after only three months of service, I was transferred from the Kings Liverpool Regiment to the South Lancashire regiment, with whom I was a despatch rider.

Fred remained with the Kings Liverpool regiment, I think it was whilst I was riding over the smooth roads of Cheshire on a new motorbike that I first got the real urge to fly, and as soon as the first opportunity came for me to transfer to the RAF, my name was down.

Fourteen weeks went by without another mention and then out of the blue came an order for me to report to Padgate RAF station where I would be interviewed by an Air Crew Selection Committee, there were lots of disappointed applicants at this place and I happened to be one of the lucky ones, but there was only a provisional acceptance for me at that time.

I was told that since I was on the small side I would have to have a cockpit check, and if I could satisfactorily reach the "rudder pedals" with my feet, I would be transferred and start training as a pilot, I would be informed of the details eventually.

As days and weeks dragged by, I was beginning to think that my name had been lost in the many files.

Another fourteen weeks had gone by when I was ordered to report to Sea land for the test.

I was taken up in a "Tiger Moth" and within ten minutes I knew that I would be given my chance to train.

Within three weeks I was in London being discharged from the Army and signed on in the RAF, three months of theory at the College in Cambridge then I was ready to try the practical part of flying.

Nearly 9 hours dual and I asked after which I was literally placed on one side until my name appeared for further training overseas.

There were schools both in Canada and Rhodesia (Africa) but I was issued with tropical kit before considering, I knew somehow it was to be Rhodesia, had I trained in Canada I would have more than likely stayed in England instead, I probably wouldn't have known the interest of Southern Rhodesia and would therefore not now be sprawled out on a bed in an Algiers Hotel.

I was roused as Fred clattered out of the bathroom

shining like a new pin.

I wasn't feeling very enthusiastic and got up with no signs of vigour.

The drinks arrived and after my bath I felt very refreshed, but I was ready for sleep, nevertheless.

Fred had a similar outlook to my own being more or less newly married, neither of us had realised the idea of being conscripted and very reluctantly accepted all the rules and regulations.

Despite that he was here and contentious and once he got heed to the ideas, he would take what came with a smile.

Before the invasion of Europe, he was transferred from Infantry to the Royal Artillery and carried the rank of Corporal.

In the signals of Royal Artillery his duty became hazardous having to maintain Telephonic communication between Operations and Head Quarters, narrowly missing death where others were less fortunate, he was mentioned in despatches.

After demobilisation we were still in touch with each other and arranged a visit and during conversation I said that I intended returning to Rhodesia and gave him my opinions.

Fred was very impressed and wanted to know more about my plans with a view to following suit, his wife was enthusiastic too and we soon got down to making some definite arrangements.

Bookings for sea passages were anything but unsatisfactory so, we looked for an alternative at a minimum cost.

Travelling by air would be alright providing we could get a suitable plane cheap enough and, I, of course have to get a Civil Flying Licence.

This did not prove too difficult, eventually we were in possession of both.

The family would stay in England until we could get Sea Passages.

It had all gone so quickly that at times it was hard to realise that we were a thousand miles or more away from home and a thousand miles nearer to the end of this journey and most certainly the most dangerous part done with, and were indeed well on our way to a new life. We only remained in Algiers the one night, I had been there several times before and I had never found it to be a very interesting place, although I know it is a popular place to some.

The ride back from town to the airfield was the most interesting period between arriving and leaving.

We could appreciate the view of the bay as seen from land, the numerous trading establishments, the type of dock workers there, and I also had the opportunity of pointing out a few places to Fred such as the Dakota House where we used to billet for the night whenever we landed there en-route during RAF service.

This was a very small hotel of about 20 rooms which had been brought into service use which had about a dozen long mission huts adjoining, all coming under the same name.

There was always a scramble to land there early in order to get one of the rooms for the night instead of having to commune with about 30 others, all strangers more or less.

Not that billeting like that was so terrible but that a private room was so rarely available to a serviceman.

Most of the traffic on the roads were mule drawn lorries, quite a number of the motor vehicles were ex-army of all shapes and sizes and probably required from some desperate Arabs who were daily risking their lives salvaging wrecked transport from the mine infected desert.

Thousands of barrels of wine lay in rows at various points along the coastal road for several miles out of town, I wondered if any would reach England, it might have arrived from France or Spain 'I don't know' but an awful lot of fat heads were cooped up there.

Booking out and taking off from Algiers was much the same as any other place, I remember the last time I was there with an RAF plane when the Americans had a lovely PX store where we got a privilege to purchase cigarettes, chocolate and gum and lots of other commodities which we were always thankful of at the time, everything this time round was French, civilian and expensive.

(11)

The next port of call would be Tunis flying at a little 1,500 ft was very uncomfortable owing to the air turbulence caused by the rugged shore, so, we tried a little higher but found very little relief.

The scenery on this leg was probably awe-inspiring although most of the time we were over the water we were always within a few miles of land.

The longest over-water period being for a duration of 23 minutes when perhaps it would have been safer to get nearer to the coast and be within gliding distance of a beach.

As the time passed the strength of the wind decreased and the bumps became less severe, during these trips when conditions were unstable, I always had in mind that perhaps this time Fred would feel sick.

During the days of preparation back in England I had given one or two sample flies with various passengers and nearly all had felt air sick before landing, here we had experienced some very trying weather and not once had Fred looked the least bit green around the gills, it hadn't occurred to me before how very disconcerting it would have been if he had been subject to nauseous feeling every time we met a bump or two, it would have been most miserable for both of us.

I remember once taking an Air Cadet youngster up for an hour whilst I practiced "Beam Approach" I was to fly at 3,500 ft the whole time and from the minute we left the runway to a couple of minutes before landing, I was flying in cloud, the poor kid never saw anything other than white vapour and was heaving his heart into a tin the whole of the hour we were up there. I have often thought about that youngster because that trip probably shattered every atom of enthusiasm he ever had about flying, and I could not disobey orders, although I would have very much liked to take him down, I felt a heel.

I would have felt the same if Fred had been sick too, but he wasn't, and Tunis was in sight 12 or 15 miles ahead.

We could not pick out the airfield, yet which is situated north of the town and in the north shore of the lake, but we soon would.

Arriving at Tunis, we found this to be a pleasant place with beautiful buildings all perfectly neat and clean, and a very efficient staff to re fuel and organise the next take off.

I had never landed at Tunis before and expected it to be a very ordinary place, it surprised me to find it a very pleasant looking place with very neat buildings and an even neater staff to refuel and attend to details for the next take off.

The dining room was pretty bedecked with numerous vases, bowls and tubs containing the most beautiful blooms of flowers one could wish for.

This is one of the few places where instead of waiters, waitresses were in attendance at the tables, actually this fact was the more outstanding to anyone who could see these waitress's ,they were certainly picked for their beauty and charm or else Tunis is a bachelor's paradise.

The uniforms they wore were typically French chic, short and tight, black and white and pleasant to look at, oh and the lunch was also up to standard and here we found it rather inexpensive, and rather nicely served, however, we were not tempted to linger and left the runway for Gabe's, where we would stay the night.

(12)

Gabe's is a place where I had often received radio bearings during flights across the med, and although I had never seen the place, I felt quite familiar with it.

Similarly, I have had many signals from Tunis, but the airfield of Tunis is called EL AOVINA and to some 4 miles NE of the town whereas Gabe's airfield is named after the town and is very close to it.

Since Algiers, the general direction of flight had been easterly, but we now had to fly due south almost, and by going from Tunis to Gabe's we were avoiding another long fly over the Med.

It would be stupid to take unnecessary risks after having got so far, as it was, we would cross about 70 miles of water, but we would be within easy reach of land.

This section to Gabe's was neither picturesque nor interesting except for the shores of the Gulf of Gabe's, these were very beautiful from the air, they looked pure and golden from the air and untouched by anything but the gentle waves of the blue Med as they brushed lightly over the sands, smoothing them off to a billiard table back.

A road and railway line follow the coast, and I

wondered what it would be like viewing the beeches from the road.

The airfield at Gabe's was nothing but a small sand landing area, fenced round with barbed wire.

At the gate was a sentry box, a few oil drums and a petrol bowser, the signal of our coming had been received at Gabe's and a handsome cab was waiting for us.

We first filled the aircraft tank in a very primitive method and spilled more than a little in doing so.

We also used a chamois to filter the petrol, as sand and water is most unwelcome in the carburettor, nevertheless, the shell representative was most helpful, he worked under difficult conditions without any decent equipment.

He had arranged for the cab to be there, it seemed he owned the cab business and took us to the most suitable accommodation in the town, there were quite a few men in uniform about that time, and we soon got an opportunity to have a word with some of them.

They were members of the French Foreign Legion, I always imagined this Legion to be 90% desperate fugitives from justice, but the majority of these were youngsters of 20 years and thereabouts, they paraded up and down in twos and threes looking for entertainment.

There were two cinema's and nothing more, I certainly didn't see anything worth staying in this town for, and, after walking along the main street once and heard the weird music pouring out of the many native cafe's and haunts and saw their occupants smoking their fantastic contraptions to the accompaniment of much talking and gesturing, I had seen everything.

There was a certain smell exceeded from all these places which is quite un describable possibly like a bake house which has been disused for some time which became dank, musty and stale.

Once out of this area, the air was clear, cool and most refreshing, and, in fact is not unusual with most seaside towns, it soon became quite chilly and so, we made for home and bedded in.

The following morning there were very few preliminaries to be done, almost everything had been prepared, a pre-flight check of the craft and we were on the move once more.

(13)

0900 GMT saw us airborne and bound for Castel Benito, the airfield at Tripoli.

Instead of taking a direct route there which would have taken us over water for about 160 miles although only a few miles off the coast, we thought it better to fly to Bon Gardena - 80 miles distant and then alter course to Castel Benito, this would only be another 5 miles further but, by doing this we would be flying overland all the way.

Between Gabe's and Castel Benito was most uninteresting, nothing in the way of unusual scenery, in fact, that region is most barren and desolate, the desert is not even colourful but grey, stony, hot and uninviting, even grim looking.

I remembered Castel Benito for the persistence of flies there, they were the fastest, trickiest and most determined flies I have ever been tormented by.

It was 11.15am when we landed, beautiful weather for flying, but the sun was high, the flies were not disappointing my anticipation, and the heat from the tarmac was very overpowering so, on the ground was not the best place to be.

Although I would rather have liked to press on from

here it was not advisable.

The next airport en-route where accommodation could be obtained was El Adem in Libya and this was too distant for us to be able to make before dark, so, we stayed the night at Castel Benito.

Castel Benito- the name of the airfield is a typical RAF place with plenty of organisation, and we had no difficulty getting food and billets which were provided by the RAF and at a very reasonable figure, the cost of the room for instance was 2/10 d each and had every facility including a bath with showers.

We were invited into the mess by some crew of a York and entertained for the evening at their expense since we had no currency of any use for that area.

Talking about old times in the forces was very interesting, and brought back some happy memories, but like myself, when I was a member of H.M. forces, all these lads were anxious to get back to civilian life.

We arranged an early call and were up with the larks, promptness in the RAF is the keyword, so, on the dot 4.30 GMT, transport at 05.00, breakfast at 05.20, a complete briefing at 06.00 and at 06.55 we were on our way to Marble Arch.

This place is now completely abandoned except for two or three Arabs who are exceedingly poor shell representatives, we had to completely supervise the re-fuelling since these men are totally incompetent.

A huge arch on the south side of the airfield is the only erection still standing, all the huts, billets, messes etc as were used by the RAF have been demolished and it is a great pity to see such waste.

There is junk of every description littered around as though a tornado had swept the place from end to end.

As a parting gesture we took a photograph of the marble arch from whence the airfield had been christened and bid goodbye to a very historic and notable battle ground where so many of those striving for supremacy had fallen.

We arrived at El Adem in the early afternoon, another RAF station spick and span with every kind of facility for the flyer.

We had good clean comfortable accommodation, and good meals were obtainable at the airfield restaurant that served the patrons by the few remaining men from the German Afrika Corp.

These men are most efficient in every way, clean, conscientious and most obliging and since all the cleaning and maintenance of the roads, quarters etc is entirely due to them, and the appearance of the place in general is a definite credit to them.

As is always the case at an RAF aerodrome every aid to the aviation community is available at El Adem, and after a complete briefing early on the 21st, we had the aircraft heading out over the desert wastes in the direction of Cairo.

Until then the trip to Cairo was the most monotonous stretch of all we had covered,

the first hour was made interesting seeing the vast numbers of wrecked vehicles, aircraft, drums and so on which had been left behind by the advancing armies.

Until one sees the apparently limitless stretches of desert and the tracks of the tanks and trucks - which are still visible after three years, one cannot imagine the magnitude of the operations undertaken by Field Marshall Montgomery and the army of which he was and still is so very proud.

Millions of miles of these tell-tale marks cover the desert, and millions of obstacles had to be overcome, obstacles made by the desert itself, thousands of yards of barbed wire can still be seen stretching in never ending lines, millions of mines are still buried there, and reliable information says that on an average five Bedouins per day are killed in the area of El Adem alone.

The war is still taking its toll even in the desert and is likely to continue to do so for years and years to come.

Flying low over a hundred miles or so was very tiring but the best advantage could be derived from the wind at low altitudes.

The only interest we found on this last hundred or so miles was the odd Arab camp which we saw.

These camps appear to be quite self-supported, and herds of sheep and goats roam the vicinity.

We took the opportunity of taking a snapshot of one of the largest camps we saw.

The mystery which persists is that for hundreds of miles around these camps, there is not the slightest trace of water.

Where the Arabs obtain their water from is still something I have still to learn.

Between El Adem and Cairo is an airfield a few miles south of Marsa Matruh, we were obliged to land here for fuel but there is very little of interest apart from the same type of battle scars which exist everywhere along the North African coast, and after a very brief stay we were all set again for Cairo.

(14)

This last leg was a nightmare, the same old desert rolled below us for mile upon mile with nothing at all to vary the scene one little bit.

It was with a sigh that we sighted Cairo West, another drome recently abandoned by the RAF, and which gave excellent services during the war and during the trooping of the unfortunates who were taken prisoners in the far East.

Thousands of ex-prisoners of war passed through Cairo West on their way home to their wives, and families, Cairo West did a great service.

We knew this drome to be only twenty-two miles from Cairo, and after a few minutes flying, the pyramids came into view, they are situated on the southwest side of Almaza where we were to land, and an alteration of course brought us to the airfield within a very short time.

A squall was developing some ten miles distant so, we were very lucky to arrive when we did, because weather of this kind in hot climates can be very disconcerting to the occupant of an aircraft as light as ours, however, we made it in time and made arrangements to have a fifty hour inspection made on the aircraft, and with the aid of a most helpful shell man, we soon organised our billets and decided to have a couple of days rest before continuing on our way.

On the way down to the hotel, we called at the office of the BOAC to see if we could manage to change some money through them, although this is not the usual procedure, but we were in need of some and fortunately for us, they obliged us with a full change value to the extent of one of our travellers cheques, they could not, however relieve us of any of our French francs which we still had and which we were finding it difficult to dispose of.

After a couple of days there, we went along to Cooks office, and there we changed enough to last us through Egypt and the Sudan, but even they could not or would not take any Francs from us, and if we had gone to a money exchange in the street we would have only got about a half of their value, so, we decided to stick with them until we got to Salisbury, Southern Rhodesia and see if we can get our money back at the proper rate of exchange.

Cairo is a very expensive place with stacks of everything one could wish for, some things were considerably cheaper than anywhere we had seen, whilst others were very similarly priced to the English standards, where there is plenty of everything in Cairo, and when I say everything, I mean everything.

Here again, French is a very popular language, and knowing only our own, we found it very difficult to get by.

Most of the shop assistants can manage a little English probably picked up from the forces, but if you were to stop a person in the street, you would most likely find that they can only speak either Arabic, French or both, unless you were lucky enough to drop across to one of the many English tourists passing through Cairo and doing a spot of shopping.

One very striking feature is the number of American cars in proportion to other makes.

There is something like 90% of the total cars in Cairo which are of American manufacture, and each one is fitted with the noisiest set of horns you ever heard, and the drivers seem to delight in sounding their horns and do so under the least provocation, so, that the din is almost frightening, and is certainly very confusing to anyone who is experiencing it all for the first time.

The fact that traffic is on the right-hand side, the road does not help one who is accustomed to seeing everyone driving on the left of the road as in Britain.

The entertainment obtainable is the best that you could wish for, though cinemas are hardly the kind to be chosen here since the weather is so stifling, and dancing is naturally very unpopular for this same reason.

Good drink can always be obtained, and the ice cream here makes this a kiddie's paradise.

The majority of the women are French, and it is an education in the art of dress to notice the elaborate styles, the care exercised in choosing their attire, and the correct shades of materials to suit particular complexions or colour of hair, the make-up is just correct and not overdone and the hairstyles are equally attractive, but above all is the abundance of jewellery worn.

There are no shoddy imitations to be seen, and an admirer of genuine stones could have a perfect field day by sitting in any cafe and observing passers-by.

Three days we spent in Cairo wondering the town admiring the shops but doing our utmost to keep expenses as low as possible, it was difficult to restrain from spending, yet before the last bill was settled in Cairo by us, we reckoned we had done very well.

By far the biggest item was the cost of the inspection made on the aircraft, and that only cost £10, so we left Cairo feeling very satisfied.

(15)

Luxor was the next place and again we had to fly over wild and desolate country. The heat was intense, the trip was bumpy, and Luxor came up on the horizon none too soon.

Along this part of the route the engine temperatures were rather high at low level and, it was not until we climbed to seven thousand feet into cooler air that they dropped to a level that I felt happy about the situation.

With a drop in temperature came the usual rise in oil pressure, this was the important factor, so, altogether it was a long and miserable trek.

Luxor is a very important place for Egyptologists owing to the many famous discoveries which have been made there in recent years.

It is situated on the bank of the Nile and on the opposite bank the West bank is **"The Valley of The Kings"** so called because so many tombs of ancient kings of Egypt have been un-earthed there.

It was here that Lord Caernarvon made the most famous discovery of all times when he discovered **Tutankhamun's tomb** in 1922, most of the contents of the tomb can now be seen in the Cairo Museum.

Luxor Airfield used to be controlled by the R.A.F but it is now almost deserted but for one or two of the officials of the native kind and the usual Shell bloke.

The heat on the ground was terrific heat, and it was a relief to get into the aircraft again and make for higher altitudes.

After a leg very much the same as the last we eventually saw Wadi Halfa where we had planned to stay the night.

On our arrival here, however that no notification of our departure from Luxor had been given, and as a result, no customs officials were on duty to attend to us, so, therefore we had to wait until they arrived.

We waited for almost an hour until one man turned up whom turned out to be most stubborn, he made it quite clear to us that he was going to make it as awkward as he possibly could, it took him every minute of the next hour to clear us and even wanted to take the typewriter away with him for safe keeping in order to be certain that we would not sell it before our departure.

That business over, we then enquired about accommodation, we were offered a lift in a shell car, but we were not allowed to accept the offer because a Taxi had arrived from town, due to an order made by the District Commissioner that, if a taxi is available it is an offence to accept a lift, so, in spite of not having ordered a taxi, we had to either use it or alternatively walk the eight or nine miles to the hotel, and the fee for the taxi was 125 piastres equal to 25/- (twenty five shillings) in English money.

The Nile Hotel is the only accommodation in Wadi Halfa, and like most businesses in this place, it is controlled by the Sudan Railways.

The charges are the most extortionate imaginable so, we quickly concluded that we must get away from here as soon as possible.

After 2 days and 3 nights the bill at the hotel was £9.18.0, (Nine Pounds and 18 shillings) so, we moved out of there and occupied an empty billet which belonged to the R.A.F.

On moving in, we made acquaintance of two trekkers who had travelled from England in an old ambulance van and were on their way to Durban in South Africa.

We bought food from the village and cooked it on a stove belonging to our newly made friends, we were happy to do this since living quite frugally, we were saving about £4. per day in expenses.

We were told by the aerodrome officer that we would not be permitted to leave Wadi Halfa unless we were in convoy with another aircraft due to no planes being allowed to fly over the Sudan unless carrying radio equipment or flying with another plane.

If we had been lucky enough to get away within a day or two, we would have been in Salisbury by the end of the month, but each morning of the next 6 days saw us still waiting for the right aircraft.

A phone call to the Control Officer of the R.A.F station at Khartoum only tended to aggravate matters, and after much pestering for permission to leave, I was refused permission to even ring the Control Officer at

Khartoum H.Q. as is frequently the case in the services.

Neither the Control Officer nor anyone else would accept responsibility for granting me permission to leave, and after a last desperate effort with the District Commissioner, we realised that we would have to wait for another aircraft in the hopes that it would come soon.

This, however, gave us the opportunity to make one or two minor adjustments to the aircraft, and there were times on the trip when we were thankful that we had made them, because two days later, we flew through some of the bumpiest of weather that we had experienced and the control cables had a very severe test.

These were the items that needed adjustment and of which we rectified at Khartoum.

At the hotel that night we saw a phenomenon which is common only to that part of the world, and which is termed 'Haboob' , this takes the form of a terrific storm comprising of large cumulus cloud which has taken dust from the desert and makes a typical "pea Souper", reducing visibility to only a few yards, and covering everything with a very fine powder.

The sky becomes obscured by the millions of particles of sand, and an ominous orange hue persists.

This awful sight precedes a vicious storm with gusts of wind and rain which lashes doors and tables about and causes havoc with the plants and shrubbery.

Whilst this was going on, our concern for the aircraft became very acute, because although we had fastened the plane down, almost anything could happen with a light craft in a wind of this type.

Fortunately for us, no damage was done and by morning the wind and rain had subsided, so, we again pressed on towards our next stop, Malakal.

(16)

After half an hour or so, a strong headwind developed, and it became policy to call in at a remote little landing field called Kosti.

A shell representative was there; he was a native living with his family in a thatched mud hut situated on the edge of a field.

His life appeared to be very primitive, a spear leaning aggressively against his door, yet to our intense surprise, there was a telephone installed inside the hut, this being for communicating with the D.C.

After re-fuelling we had a word with the D.C over the phone, he sent a telegram off to Malakal to say we had called at Kosti and we didn't stay longer than was necessary and went on our way over land that was changing from desert to a more vegetated area with plenty of water available and many more signs of native life.

At Malakal the same question about convoy arose with the airfield officer, but after a little persuasion, he agreed to sign the logbook and allow us to depart at 04.45 pm the following day for Juba, the last stopping place in the Sudan.

We were anxious to get through Juba, because once

we had left there, no rule of convoying was in force, so we were able to go any way we desired and, at any time to suit ourselves.

Crossing the Nile for the last time we could see a marked change of terrain, there was such dense forest below extending for hundreds of square miles that we were on watch for any small clearing which would enable us to get down in comparative safety should we be so unfortunate as to have engine failure at this stage of the trip, even then there would be very little chance of survival for the jungle below would no doubt be infested with all sorts of wild beasts, and, due to proximity of the equator, there is little doubt that the place would be fever ridden.

We had no means of self-defence other than a fairly large and sturdy knife, and it was with as much relief as when we crossed the Med that we saw Juba come in to view, a very small place with one natural runway, really nothing more than a cutting in the forest, we wasted no time here, and after scaring several native women and in nothing more than a cloth wrapped around the hips we landed.

This was the first experience of "Remote Africa" although they had no bones in their noses and fires burning ready to burn us alive it was quite an unusual place where the natives obviously were not used to many white faces, I now wonder how Dr David Livingstone (The British Explorer) felt when arriving in Africa for the first time and the many African villages he encountered on his travels back in the 1800's.

We topped up with fuel here and were on our way in no time, there was no red tape as such here just a form to sign and details of the plane.

We were drawing closer to Southern Rhodesia and only a few countries left to pass through.

We went through every other country basically in the same way which are listed here in order of flying: -

After Juba we flew to Soroti (Uganda) today.

Kisumu (Kenya)

Tabora (Tanzania)

Kasama (Zambia)

Lusaka (Zambia Capital)

Salisbury (Rhodesia) now Zimbabwe.

From Soroti it was very much arriving at listed drome's as these were proper cities and buildings where we off loaded and stayed in fresh smart accommodation for a day or two with fresh running water and good English food.

The airdromes were up to scratch and fuel was easily available when we needed it.

Juba was the only small air strip we encountered which was a one-off small landing strip in the bush.

(17)

Exciting times were ahead of us and our futures as we drew nearer and nearer to our final landing spot in Southern Rhodesia.

We left Manchester on the 7th of May 1947 and arrived at our final destination (Southern Rhodesia) on the 8th of June 1947 after a total of 15 flying days and some considerable delay at Wadi Halfa by the Egyptian authorities.

As we touched down at Belvedere Airport in Salisbury was quite jubilant as my very dear friends were there to greet us amongst others, I befriended during my training days before the war where I was billeted to become an air pilot before the war broke out in Europe but this time, staying with them as guests.

I didn't think I would see this day emerge, both Fred and I were so relieved and relaxed as we sat down with our new adopted family over food, and drink in their beautiful home explaining all our days of adventure, excitement and moments of anxiety and fear of things going wrong.

This was my dream come true at long last after such a long time of planning.

We finally unpacked our luggage this time a little

more permanently and as soon as we could we wrote home with the excitement that we had arrived safely, these were quite anxious times for our families back home and the relief for us all was quite tremendous, they didn't know if we were alive or not.

We finally got settled in and was ready to send for the family as soon as we could get shipping organized from the UK to Cape Town in South Africa, then it was organising trains from Cape Town to Rhodesia unfortunately this took many months to arrange which ended up exactly a year later to the day, so, it wasn't plain sailing as we wanted it to be.

I hadn't seen my family for just over a year, but the good news was I had work and was able to secure a more permanent place for us to live once more as a family.

They arrived on the 8th June 1948 a whole year almost to the day by sea to Cape Town then a train to Bulawayo in Rhodesia and then on to Salisbury (the capitol) where we planned to settle, we met them all in such exciting and happy moments, we shall never forget, I couldn't believe how my boys had grown so much in a year.

Talking about how things were back home in Manchester, how life was so hard to cope with and how sad it was too, leaving family behind not knowing if we would ever see them all again.

We could now look forward to a wonderful life in Africa and enjoy the fruits of opportunities that lay ahead of us.

Both Fred his family and I stayed forever true

friends.

Alan and Peter enjoying their life on their African Farm.

**Below is a speech of an "Air Force Commander"
officially opening a Hall named after Daniel Murray.**

*Mrs Murray, Group Captain Penton ladies and
gentlemen.*

*We have congregated on this fine morning to perform
a task which is both pleasant and nostalgic.*

*Our purpose is to name and declare officially open the
building which you see behind me.*

*This building is not a new one but has been brought to
its present state of combined efforts of members of the
Volunteer Reserve.*

*What has been achieved here has been epitomises the
spirit of the Rhodesian Air Force as we know it.*

*As I contemplate this building, I am reminded of an
aphorism with which some of you may be familiar.*

*We the willing, led by the unknowing are doing the
impossible for the ungrateful.*

*We have done so much for so long with so little that we
are now qualified to do anything with nothing at all.*

I feel that it has justifiable application on this occasion.

*The building now occupied by the "Voluntary Reserve"
training centre was originally constructed as the station
hospital, Cranbourne for No 1 Rhodesian Air Training
group during the second world war.*

*Since the original requirement fell away the complex
has been used as a Maternity Home, a Hostel and also
stood derelict until the Voluntary Reserve got to grips
with the situation, and, so the wheel has come full circle
with "Blue Jobs" once again in possession.*

As you are aware, the centre is shared by three

Voluntary Reserve Squadrons and floor space is, thus, at a premium.

Virtually at the time that the centre was re-occupied the need has been apparent for a suitable venue for larger gatherings.

I have no doubt that covetous eyes have been cast many times on this hall behind me which started its life as a temporary hospital ward.

I emphasize temporary for it must delight the heart of a parsimonious treasury to see a building which had a design life of 5 years in use some 35 years later.

In any event I am told that the building has been used "spasmodically" in the intervening years as a Judo club of which I have no doubt that it was also used painfully.

I suppose we should be thankful that it was not a Kung-Fu Club whose members might have seen fit to demolish it with their bare hands before they finally vacated it.

Having been taken over, a great deal of self-help work was put into converting it into a meeting hall.

For the uninitiated, "self-help "is one of those glorious euphemisms which cover a multitude of nefarious activities.

What it really means is that you help yourself to whatever you need from whatever source by whatever means to achieve your objective.

I need hardly say that the Air Force has developed a certain degree of expertise in this field, and I would accordingly like to thank the numerous unknown-and the unknowing - benefactors who have assisted so generously with this project.

It is just as well that walls cannot speak -or the whole

building would probably have been seized as evidence long before now.

No grant - in- aid or any other official money was allocated for these renovations, by the Air force.

Naming a building is invariably a vexatious task, and as a result many end up with meaningless coined names or by being named after someone who did little or nothing to assist the projects and deserved the honour less.

I am happy to say that neither of these possibilities applies in the present case.

This hall is to be named most fittingly after one of the "Stalwarts" of the (V R) Voluntary Reserve, the late Air Lieutenant Daniel Murray, who was called to higher service on the 25th of February 1975.

Dan's air force career began during the last war of WW2 and firstly volunteered for Army service of the outbreak of war in 1939 and then transferred to the RAF in 1941.

His association with Rhodesia and possibly with these very buildings began in December 1942 when he was posted to Cranbourne barracks from Belvedere for further flying training on Harvards.

Some few months later he was posted back to the UK for further training on the Whitley.

He was one of those brave men who piloted Horsa Gliders during the Airborne invasion of Europe.

Thereafter, he was posted to operational transport duties, both over France and Germany and latterly in the Middle East and India until his eventual de-mobilisation in June 1946.

He obviously found post-war England not to his liking and having had a taste of Rhodesia, his next move was predictable.

What was not predictable was his method of travel, although it was entirely in keeping with his character and spirit.

Sea Births were virtually impossible to obtain so, Dan purchased a single Engine "Autocrat" so together with another colleague got Airborne on the 9th May 1947.

His flight plan sounds like extracts from a Gazetteer!

Dan Murray Hall named after him with Gladys Murray and all 4 boys.

Gladys receiving the remembrance award named after Daniel for all his hard work he put in for the RRAF.

BARTON - DERBY- LYMPNE - TOUSSUS LE NOBLE - LIMOGES - TOULOUSE -PERPIGNON - BARCELONA - VALENCIA - ALGIERS - TUNIS - GABES - CASTEL - BENITO - MARBLE ARCH - EL ADEM -MERSA MATRUH - CAIRO - LUXOR - WADI HALFA - KHARTOOM - KOSTI-MALAKAL - JUBA - SOROTI - KISUMU - TABORA - KASAMA - LUSAKA - SALISBURY, (BELVEDERE) in RHODESIA his final destination where he landed on the 8th June 1947.

After a total of 15 flying days with some considerable delays at WADI HALFA by the Egyptian authorities plus stop overs in all taking 32 days.

HIS CAREER

Like many others Daniel took to the soil first as a Farm Assistant and later on as Manager of Chikurubi Estates where they farmed Tobacco, Maize and Timber 15 miles on the Northern side of Salisbury.

He then worked for a Count Delano a Spanish Count of Bluewater's Estate in Bromley which was 30 miles out of Salisbury on the Eastern side, they farmed Tobacco and Maize.

Dan then went on to buy a farm (Waterford Farm) in a partnership with a colleague but after a while he had to sell his half of the business due to health reasons.

During the early 1960's he developed his own "Shoe Manufacturing business" which was highly successful as there were no shoe manufacturers in Rhodesia apart from a small outlet in a place called Gwelo.

He became one of the top manufacturers in the whole country he supplied to all the top shoe shops throughout Rhodesia, this was named G & D Shoes, taking his wife's first letter of her Christian name (Gladys) and his first name (Daniel).

Gladys, Dan's wife became the backbone of G & D Shoes where she did all the buying and visits throughout the country to customers, also a very tough business orientated women was highly successful later on in her life where she became a Chief Executive for a very large Departmental Store.

All their shoes were exclusively designed for them by an ex-air force colleague who served with him during the war so, with Daniel's influence he came out to Rhodesia to also make a new life for himself and his family.

Daniels business flourished, he was an extremely hard worker and very much a technical person with a business head on his shoulders.

It didn't take Dan long to find his way back to his first love so, he attested into the Voluntary Reserve in 1960.

He was one of those personalities often found in the Air Force whose employment was a way of life rather than a mere job.

He served with 103 Squadron and the consistency of his service is illustrated by the fact that he maintained one of the highest rates of call-up of all the squadron's members until he passed on.

Leadership by example was an outstanding characteristic of Dan's service.

Whenever there was practical work to be done, he would be at the forefront of the activity, suitably armed with a paint brush, hammer or other implements.

He had the distinction of being the oldest member of the V R., but this was never a limitation to any of his force activities.

As an example, he invariably featured as one of the top three scorers in the squadron's musketry exercises.

Dan is not with us today in person, but his spirit certainly is.

We are very happy and honoured that his wife and family are with us today as guests of honour.

This hall and what it symbolises will be a lasting tribute to our friend and comrade-in-arms, and I have now great pleasure in declaring the "DAN MURRAY HALL" officially open.

Gladys & Dan on their farm with all 4 boys with Arnot their
Donkey and YoYo the cat.

Author's Note

Both Dan and Gladys became highly respected and well known in business top circles within the country which included Dan's full-time participation for the Rhodesian Air Force which was his first love.

Gladys and Dan had 2 boys born in the United Kingdom (Alan & Peter) and went on to have another 2 boys born in Rhodesia (Christopher & Leslie.)

Alan the first born took to the air like his father and served in the Rhodesian Royal Air Force becoming involved with the Rhodesian Bush War at the time, he also went on to be a very highly influential business man owning a company named "Murray Enterprises" and then branched into a Jewellery manufacturers "Alan Murray Jewellers." Alan ran this business very successfully until the 1980's where he and his wife and family sold up and left for a new life in South Africa.

The other 3 brothers went their separate ways in their careers, Peter being a Plastics Technical Manager in Rhodesia for many years also moved to South Africa to continue his career in the Plastics Industry and Christopher running his own Safari Company (Prima Luce Tours and Safari's.) in the Kruger National Park, South Africa where he still runs this today.

Leslie the youngest was involved in wildlife and ran many Lion parks in Rhodesia for a while, he also owned a Gold Mine in Rhodesia but has now retired in the United Kingdom.

Daniel never let a challenge pass him by throughout his life and even having Rheumatic Fever at the young age of 14 years which weakened his heart, it never deterred him.

He then had another Rheumatic Fever attack at the age of 40 years old where the doctors insisted, he gave up farming, which he reluctantly did but, continued through his life taking challenges with excitement.

He never let anything get in his way but the strenuous work on a farm was not good for his health which is when he started up the shoe manufacturing business.

Dan continued with the shoe business into the 1970's but his doctors once again decided he should retire and slow down which is when he decided for health reasons to sell up and retire.

Dan Murray died of a heart attack, he was taken from us far too soon, he had so much more to achieve in his lifetime, we all know that he would have carried on and on but at a young age of 63 years his "plane" landed for the last and final time.

Dan's ashes were scattered over RRAF (Rhodesian Royal Air Force Base "New Sarum Airfield" close to the Dan Murray Hall named in his honour.

He now flies high in the skies where he just loved to be. Gladys died in South Africa in her mid-80's.

Both of them now gone, the family have such special memories as two of the most amazing and influential people in our lives.

I myself as a family member am so proud to have been part of their lives and shall always remember them with such honour and respect.

"*Wings Over Africa*" has been an even greater honour, for me to put together and write, and to travel with him through time on his amazing journey from England to Africa during those early years.

Susan Murray
September 2020.

www.ingramcontent.com/pod-product-compliance
Lightning Source LLC
Chambersburg PA
CBHW021128130626
46554CB00002B/915